The Way to Begin, 2nd Edition

Get your story out of your head

By

Michael W. Harkins

The Method That Guides You
From Idea to Story!

Copyright 2025 Michael W. Harkins, all rights reserved.
Second edition, May 2025

ebook ISBN: 978-0-9965672-9-9
print ISBN: 978-0-9965672-7-5

Except as permitted under the U.S. Copyright Act of 1976, no part of this publication may be reproduced, distributed, or transmitted in any form by any means, or stored in a database or retrieval system, without the prior written permission of the author.

Excerpts from Everybody's Fool, Get Shorty, and Move to Fire used for educational purposes and all rights are reserved by their owners.

Cover design by Writesite - Story and Pictures, 'Write Everyday' illustration by Tomoko Sekitani and M.W. Harkins

For all inquiries contact
info@storyandpictures.com

A brief note about The Way to Begin 2nd edition

I first wrote The Way to Begin as an accompanying guide for a community education class I created and taught at a local junior college. Feedback and reviews were positive, with attendees especially appreciating the guidance and insights that, for many, finally got them beyond the obstacles blocking them from writing a story. This edition is slightly expanded, with some additional words devoted to character development, editing, and plot, and a few general, necessary updates.

Introducing The Way to Begin	1
You Need More Than An Idea	9
Decision Time	37
Your Creative Log Line	49
Author-Worthy Prose	61
Tomorrow is not your moment	97
About Michael W. Harkins	103

Introducing The Way to Begin
Getting from idea to words on paper

You have an idea for a story, sparked by something you saw or read, or by someone you know. It might have bubbled up out of your imagination and you can't think of anything else. You've worked on it in your head for weeks, months, or years, and you've amassed boxes and megabytes of research.

You want to write that story. You really, really want to write that story... but...

You just don't know how to begin, how to actually put pen to paper or fingertips to keyboard and write your story's opening pages. You're ready, you're sure, or maybe you're not ready but you are looking for that 'something' to help you move forward.

Ideas are not not books. They are not short stories, memoirs, biographies, screenplays, stage plays, self-help books, magazine articles, or blog posts (and they are not products, services, or careers, either). Ideas are a place called Start, an insight, occasionally a solution, or a dream experienced while awake. Ideas are seeds of opportunity, with the potential to grow into something beautiful, meaningful, revolutionary, incendiary, lyrical, moving, or comical. They are flashes, glimpses of something that entices, a light from deep within a cave, sirens that beckon the curious and the explorer.

Ideas are easy. Putting words together in an organized manner to convey something is hard, especially for new or still learning writers (don't be discouraged — it's a lifelong process).

About me and The Way to Begin's origins

Often when someone is made aware that I'm a writer there comes some variation of this quick, unsolicited share: "I have an idea for a book..." or "I have a great idea for a movie..." and then, "I just don't know how to start..."

I empathize. I've been there. Seeking information from someone who has it — asking me, because I'm a writer — is a legitimate step to finding out basic information on how to begin. While I believe there are only a few absolutes in this world, I also believe that everyone carries at least one 'book' within them but few actually write it.

I can't guarantee that you will write anything at all after learning The Way to Begin's process. I can't chain you to a chair and shackle your wrists to your keyboard. But I can give you what you need to develop and understand your story and its characters, and clear away any obstacles that have prevented you, until now, from writing those first few pages. After those pages comes hard work, dedication, and story telling. For now, all I want to say is that writing a complete piece of work — short story, article, novella, or book — is a process of learning and doing that can't happen until you commit to those first few pages.

I've been a professional writer, designer, and creative guy for over four decades. I've been very lucky and had some great opportunities, but I spent countless hours reading, learning, and writing, often night and day.

Over the course of my career I've created and written every form of story, nonfiction to fiction, corporate training guide to magazine cover story. This isn't an attempt to impress you, it's to assure you that I've learned how to write. If I can learn, so can you, and I can teach you how to start.

My path to professional writing has been unusually winding, includes only a couple of years of college, but also includes unique adventures, a willingness to explore (literally and figuratively) and never ending quests to read for pleasure and for intellectual gain. (BTW, I don't recommend skipping post-high school education, nor do I recommend following the kind of winding path I roamed). Many of my students experienced some of that same kind of path. Many adults come to writing when they've reached the place where they have time to do what they've always wanted to do, or promised themselves they would do. Younger writers, in or after college and university, discover a yearning to share views, perspectives, opinions, and stories in ways that capture someone's long term attention, evokes emotions, and challenges readers to consider alternate perspectives.

New writers benefit the most from the The Way to Begin (although it can also assist any writer working through plotting or character challenges). The process is a creative mix of logic, analysis, and imagination, but as in every endeavor it is only one important tool in what should be a lifetime of continually filling a writer's toolbox. The Way to Begin should be one of many writing books on your physical and digital bookshelves.

Helping new writers achieve their important, rewarding 'start' is the major reason The Way to Begin exists at all. I developed it decades ago when teaching video production and scriptwriting in San Francisco. Class after class, when given the opportunity to choose a subject for their first documentary-type assignment, many students chose the same subjects.

With each new class I began to use the commonality of what I knew was coming\. Classes were downtown, which exposed students daily to several observable, societal challenges, especially homelessness (as it was called then; the favored term now is "unhoused"). It followed, then, that every semester multiple students chose to do their assignments on homelessness. I used that choice to develop a new approach that guided students in breaking down and understanding the complex web — and as an issue, homelessness is a massive web — confronting anyone who wanted to write and produce a video report on 'something' regarding homelessness. Working with students to help them understand how to recognize the complexity of a subject, to find and focus on a cohesive, consistent point of view from which to build their story, was the catalyst for the Way to Begin.

I think it's also important that you know my personal reasons for sharing the Way to Begin method: The world needs competent writers and storytellers. To facilitate their creation, other writers who can teach writing competency need to step up. Understand that it will always be work, but it doesn't have to be insurmountable, you just need to know a few important things before you start.

There is a way to begin, a method that eases the difficult transition of your idea into your story's opening pages. If you follow the guidance and do the work, you *will* get your story out of your head. That act of putting words to paper or screen makes it more likely that you'll keep writing until you've finished a complete draft, a huge accomplishment. The important caveat here is that The Way To Begin is one tool in a toolbox that you must fill with an endless gathering of lessons — self taught, in classes, or by mentors — about character development, plots, and the craft of writing.

A note about this new edition: I've expanded the Author-worthy Prose chapter to include some additional guidance on character development, style and pacing, and how TWTB's approach can make you a better storyteller no matter your platform of choice. Storytelling is what writing is at every stage. Matter of fact, stage is the perfect word to equate with building a story. Mastering mechanics and craft are paramount for success, but they must facilitate the *telling* of your story.

Time is an arrow that only moves in one direction, which means change happens, and that means it's hard to keep cultural references timely once those references have become part of the record. The included 'first page' examples from other books are the same in this new edition as in TWTB's first edition. Reading or purchasing printed books might be waning, but the number of books released every year remains massive, and making attempts to update those examples to include more recent books is impracticable. The original examples remain not just because of that impracticability, but because they remain worthy of study, although I may yet choose to update the examples at some point.

Now read, write, and work hard, so that we may all benefit from reading *your* story!

MWH

You Need More Than An Idea
Ideas aren't enough

Every story's elements are the same no matter the intended final form, be it novel, screenplay, memoir, or featured podcast. That should be reassuring, because The Way to Begin works for all of those.

There are writers who know where their story is going, writers who know some of where it's going, writers who just start writing, and writers who really, really want to start and just don't know how. All writers eventually develop their own way to begin, but The Way to Begin method teaches how to narrow and define story choices, build characters (which also apply to nonfiction projects!), and reveals how to elevate your writing to author-worthy prose.

Why is the idea-to-pages transition difficult?

An idea will only carry you so far… which is one reason it's sometimes so hard to write that story which, as an idea, seemed so good.

An idea is a cloud. It's ephemeral, without reference points, impressive in size and shape, but so lacking in substance it changes shape and density at every moment even as it remains a cloud.

Everything is perfect in your head. Your story idea is exciting, your characters are alive, fully developed, all perfect, as are your grammar, punctuation, and sentence construction. The internal perfection of an idea can be so exciting that it compels you to the keyboard, energized, but writing that just-right opening line or finding those just-right words seems impossible.

The writer reaches a "Now what?" place, a dead end, or Multiple Choice Junction. It's okay, because except for a figurative handful of people, all writers have at some point arrived at those dreaded locales. Work hard and, perhaps with an assist from The Way to Begin, you'll eventually look back fondly on when you finally began.

An idea has no details until YOU decide details. It is only through examining the idea that you understand how incomplete it is. No story idea has any staying power, any logic, any magic, any hope of being shared with an appreciative audience until it's all out of your head, because the head-to-paper portal is critical. It challenges you with question after question about your story: Where's it going? What about this? What about...? Several things occur when you commit to writing those first words, then sentences, then paragraphs, then pages. You quickly understand where the empty parts of your idea are, what's needed to fill them.

The subsequent frustration of not being able to sustain that initial surge can stop a writer after only a few paragraphs. The inherent incompleteness of a story idea is the usual obstacle, but other causes include:

- A lack of or weak foundational writing skills, grammar, punctuation, sentence construction;
- Unfamiliarity with basic story composition, plot, pacing, character development, etc.;
- *Research overload*, my term for when a writer has invested so much research time into a subject that the volume of collected information overwhelms the ability to choose the story's entry point;

- Stasis, a *deer in the headlights* inertia resulting from thinking too much about the time, effort, and work necessary to write a book or complete story (very similar to research overload).

Here's a suggestion to alleviate the *thinking too much about the time, effort, and work necessary to write a book*. One 'filled' sheet of paper set to one-inch margins, double-space lines, and 12-point Times New Roman font (standards you should adopt now, btw), contains slightly more than 300 words. **Write just one page in that format every day and in only six months you could have 50,000 words.** That's a book.

Basic English and writing classes, and disciplined self-instruction in creative writing, grammar, and punctuation, will improve your overall writing, but there are two books that I label as must reads. The first, physically small yet loaded with solid, foundational writing wisdom, which every writer should read no matter that writer's station in life or mastery of craft, is **Strunk & White's** *The Elements of Style.*

There is a bit of a "meh..." attitude within pockets of the writing community that question the 21st century relevance of a writing style guide first written in 1920.

I am a professionally competent writer. The Elements of Style contributed mightily to my competence, and whenever I re-read it I find its value and relevance undeniable. It is to be read, absorbed, and read again every handful of years. It is a concise, succinctly presented volume of how to write well. It teaches what active writing is, compares it to passive writing, provides absorbable examples of good vs. mediocre writing, and demonstrates how to avoid composing poorly structured, grammatically and punctually incorrect prose.

There are now many, many good books similar to The Elements of Style, and while I still prefer its direct, easily understood guidance, I do have another more recent favorite: 2019's ***Dreyer's English***. Benjamin Dreyer, former chief copy editor at Random House, wrote a spot on, humorous book that entertains as it teaches. It sits beside my frayed Elements of Style and Chicago Manual of Style.

Those three volumes are especially important resources in this time of instant access to knowledge. Though there are some legitimate drawbacks of having too much instant access to an overabundance of information, a more pressing problem is hordes of instant online expertise providers. Many of those self-positioned teachers and experts often lack the required experience and acumen of a bonafide teacher. This became clear to me some time ago after discussions with a potential client about writing new copy for a website. This person was considering writing it themselves, and referenced an online copywriting course developed by a then in-demand, online copywriter. "His style is fresh and a lot of companies are using him. And his course is not expensive."

So, I checked it out, went to the website, read the introduction. Here is the landing page's first sentence: "Most copywriting sinks or swims right out of the gate."

That sentence is a mixed metaphor. A horse, greyhound, or any other animated creature, including a human, can falter, win or lose a race right out of the gate. But the phrase 'sinks or swims' doesn't help the writer with what he or she is attempting to convey, because it has nothing to do with 'out of the gate,' as that has nothing to do with water. Lest you think I'm being too harsh or narrow minded, that sentence is exactly the kind of composition that would be marked as incorrect in the most basic writing quiz. Its existence on a site that purports to teach copywriting skills, fee based or not, is abhorrent, because it's just so wrong and many new writers wouldn't realize it.

Any competent writing instructor wants you to write well. Conversely, you want to be taught by someone who knows what he or she is talking about.

Beginning writers are often so driven by the quest to write a story (I know, I know, that IS the whole point). I assure you that when agents, editors, publishers, reviewers, readers, and clients read work with mistakes in grammar, punctuation, or sentence structure, the mistakes can negate the story's originality or inventiveness. Read The Elements of Style, Dreyer's English, or both!

A momentary digression: "What is a writer?"

Let's do some introspection before we move on. What do these words mean to you: I write; I am writing; I am a writer.

Consider this comparison: I drive a truck vs. I am a truck driver. The first statement can include anyone who uses a truck of any kind for work or as a personal vehicle, but whose livelihood does not necessarily rely upon driving a truck. The second statement usually refers to a credentialed or licensed professional who operates a truck as a livelihood.

Big difference. Now, read these statements to find the one, or those, that apply to you:

— "I write because I…":

have always wanted to.

have always wanted to try.

have always told stories.

have always said I will some day.

have always wanted to be some kind of a writer.

have always written.

But, if nothing above applied to you, why are you reading this book?

I want to write about x.

I think I have a great story idea.

I want to write a movie.

I want to learn how to write.

Not knowing why you want to write doesn't preclude you from becoming a fine writer. We're all aware of media/Internet-fueled instant success, but management of your expectations is highly encouraged. If you have not been writing diligently, every day, for as long as you can remember, that doesn't mean you shouldn't work incredibly hard and strive to be the next Colson

Whitehead, J.K Rowling, Jonathan Franzen, Lee Childs, Zadie Smith, or Stephen King, but it is unlikely that you will be, and you should be okay with that realization. You don't have to have massive 'commercial' or critical success to be a writer. Writers are no different than other creative artists — they do whatever they need to so they can write. Many writers also teach, others work at whatever they can, and many barely earn a living wage.

Not a great motivational piece, I know, but the upside to living now is that there have never been more opportunities to share your work, be published, and find readers.

Writers write for many reasons, but rarely because they want to be famous or wealthy. Writers write for the same reason a painter paints, a musician plays, an actor acts — because creating resonates with them, because writers can't not write, and all of them want to be better, to work and improve constantly.

Write for the right reason.

A book about your family tree can be the right reason, as can your spy novel, how-to make gnocchi, or your family's memoir... any reason at all, as long as you're writing to write.

A brief note about reading

It might seem obvious to many of us that to be a writer also means to be a reader.

But, surprisingly, it's not the case. Upon hearing that I was a magazine writer, someone once asked me, "What about writing a book, is that a big deal? Because I have this idea..." and when I asked what he liked to read, he replied that he didn't read much, and he didn't write.

Hooo-kay...

Read. 'Nuff said.

About that idea...

An idea is many things. It's a cloud, or a sketch, a seed that might, or might not, grow.

It's not even a plan (yet). Think of it as an invitation, from you to you, to explore. Ideas, like clouds and seeds, need **catalysts, acts or actions that generate transformation** into a next stage: seed to flower, or cloud to rain, then rainbow, thunderstorm, tornado, snow, river, land, food, life, destruction, death.

For the writer, those catalysts result from one thing: ***decisions***.

Decisions are the beginning of the process that transform an idea or ideas into a bonafide story.

A temperature change, warm air confronting cold air, air condensing into small particles of ice, these catalysts start that transformation process. It's analogous to developing a story, and you can discern that from the active words in the preceding sentence: change, confront, condense. Verbs and other words that convey action or movement are the very same things we — and by extension, characters — all deal with our entire lives. We change, we confront, we (and fate) do things that are the catalysts of our lives.

As a writer, your decisions are the catalysts that affect and transform ideas. They transform your idea's potential into what you need it to be: a car, statue, person, house, company, forest, castle, gun, outer space, a concert, a riot, a car, a yacht, inner space, time and place…

Your decisions create the catalysts, then those catalysts' subsequent **transformations create, and lead to, actions and consequences**, whether those actions and consequences come from, or happen to, people, animals, or a literal environment like a city or house, or figurative one, like the mood shift in a courtroom or a societal shift after a contentious election. The writer's decisions about *story elements* are the transformations that make a story possible.

Here is one of my own soulless definitions of story: A story is a listing or listings of actions, reactions, and consequences, all influenced by **context**, within a period of time.

Wait; what's context?

For our writing purposes, context is backstory and influences.

Context

The definition of context most applicable to creative writing is: *the interrelated conditions in which something exists or occurs; group of conditions that exist where and when something happens*

Someone whose existence is formed and informed by being raised in a small town environment will have a worldview that is vastly different than someone raised in a city. The same things that distinguish one person's life from another person's life — growing up on a farm, growing up in the city, growing up as an only child, growing up with brothers and sisters, etc. — are the things that *influence* your story's characters. *Characters influence other characters*, just as our lovers, family, friends, and enemies (perceived and real) influence us.

Backstory

Backstory is what the writer knows and the reader may or may not need to know. **Everything has backstory**, because in the real world and the made-up world, all existence is a three act play, and the arrow of time never stops, and never goes in reverse. When we meet a character or come into a story scene, a multitude of experiences, paths, and incidents have led to that character's or scene's entry point. That's backstory.

Our every moment is one of three acts: going, being, leaving. For a reader, a character comes into existence the first time he or she is described on the page, but for the writer, that character, just like us actual carbon-based lifeforms, 'came' from somewhere, even if the author doesn't explain where 'came from' is, or was.

Here's an example based on a nice moment of conversation I had with Camie Foust, a very special friend and actress who in the earliest days of my writing career shared wonderful insights about the development of character.

We were watching a hospital-themed TV show. As two doctors talked in a hospital corridor, a continuing stream of nurses and other characters entered and exited in the background of the scene. Those background actors who populate scenes are known as extras, a term with which many of us are familiar. They create the visual fabrics of crowded sidewalks, restaurants, bars, etc. They rarely have any lines, never more than a few (or they have to be paid differently) and we barely take note of them.

In the scene, a nurse came out of a room, walking away from the camera and down the corridor. I noticed that a smidgen of her slip was drooping an inch or so beneath the hem of her uniform skirt, and I said something to the effect of, "Huh, guess someone in wardrobe missed that."

Camie said, "No, that's not a mistake. The actor did that on purpose."

She went on to explain what I already knew as a developing writer but hadn't applied to what I was seeing. The extra was certainly a professional (this was a very successful, highly rated show) and, like all actors, either knew her character's backstory or, in this instance because she was an extra, created her own. Whether because of a hurried morning getting to work, in hour eleven of a twelve hour shift, or simply because the character had too much work to be concerned with a slip of the slip, the actor had created a backstory that was unknown to the viewers but had led to her brief appearance in the story itself.

That actor knew that to convey an honest, truthful representation of that character, the character had been alive and in that world for years, and for the moment we observed her, we were seeing her where she was now, and she was on her way to somewhere else.

And she had neither time nor inclination to check her slip.

She had been going somewhere, she had arrived somewhere, and she was going somewhere else. Her three act life is literal and figurative. Her personal three act life journey could be that she studied to become a nurse's assistant (going); is a nurse's assistant (being); and is going to night school to become a registered nurse (leaving).

For a reader, a character first comes into existence the first time he or she, or it, is described on the page, but for the writer that character came from somewhere, even if the writer doesn't explain where 'came from' is. And as an extra note about the context of time and place, nurses and other medical workers in a hospital environment now where scrubs more than any other work uniform. Now the context of that character insight above is that it's from a different time than now (the '80s, to be exact).

Like getting to work, eating dinner, getting the kids to bed, going to bed with a mistress, reading in a library, stealing a car, all of the elements of life that 'actual' people experience, your characters also experience. The difference — one of the differences — is that the reader or viewer of a character may not know, or doesn't have to know, which of the three acts we're in. Character's lives are no different than our own, and both are very much like one of the striking attributes of physics: no matter how deeply physicists dive into the structure of everything, they never reach the point where they can't go any deeper. Taking apart each level of elements and molecules and atoms leads to yet more levels. For humans, for the characters and locations and times in our stories, we see only the bits and pieces of their existence. A man going to the restaurant, having lunch in the restaurant, and leaving when he's finished to go somewhere else, those are three acts, but each one of those acts is itself its own three act life. As the creator of worlds — or as the world's reporter — the writer chooses which act and how much of it creates the story.

When it's the time and place to do it, the writer includes elements of backstory. It is the history, short or long, that gets that character to a place which is then shared with us. Some writers do very elaborate backstories, while other writers may create it as they write. For the vast majority of beginning or new creative writers, I recommend creating and writing some kind of backstory not just for your characters, but for the story itself — knowing what has already happened makes it much easier to begin writing the story.

When combined, context (life/location/events your character has been exposed to) and backstory (a family tree, mom, dad, orphan, ancestors) are what make your characters, their actions and decisions, true to life and believable.

Take a moment to consider how family history and life experiences, like bullying, a loving upbringing, a hurricane, arson, a dysfunctional family, mental illness, privilege, poverty, chance, a wildfire, etc., affect people. Nothing is insignificant, especially if you are creating your own story universe.

Let's go back to those decisions that create catalysts and transform your ideas.

"Okay, I need to make decisions, but, **how do I decide?**"

Decisions are the magic / the bonus / the power of being a writer. The easiest decisions come from familiarity, i.e., an ex-cop who wants to write crime stories, a CPA with a background in international finance writes a story about a French banker who stumbles across a CIA-involved, international investment scam... The other decisions come from what interests you: what do *you* like?

Familiarity — What you know

Familiarity has its positives and negatives. The negatives can and must be overcome by willing yourself to enter those dark, sometimes intimidating empty places that exist, because what you're familiar with often can't carry an entire story.

Imagination and your willingness to let imagination guide you are the torches that illuminate those foreboding spaces. The torch light shines through walls, shows you paths, reveals the magic doorway to let in the light of what you need, what you seek: a lost hero, found love, a stray animal, a little boy, a little girl, the

King of England, an assassin, treasure, poison, a vampire (along with zombies, very popular), a sexy vampire (always popular)…

That with which you are familiar — you're a cop, cook, gardener, therapist, doctor, you've lost the use of your legs, you're a mom, father, won the lottery, worked your way up from poverty to world's best known author of stories about wizards and children — is a convenient, legitimate start. It may, indeed, carry you through much of your story as an autobiography, memoir, or a fictional version based on your life. But even with details of your life to guide you, you still have to create all the things that successful writers create: plot, tension, drama, pathos, the elements of story that build the bridge from the book to the reader.

Research

And so, familiarity or not, there is research to be done… and research is seductive.

Research is a seductive addiction. It's invaluable but, like reading, 'researching' is much, much easier and more enjoyable for most of us than writing (hence the seduction). It must be managed (like expectations) and integrated into the writing process itself.

It does legitimately require reading, but the best research is that which places you physically in an actual environment itself. Within that environment is (almost always) everything you need to populate all the levels of your story, from the feel of the wind to the smell of the air, from the sounds of traffic or conversations to people's sideways glances, smirks, looks of disappointment or triumph, people's gaits, the sounds of gravel underfoot, the perceived vs. actualities of spaces (that football field populated by gargantuan multi-millionaire men that the majority of us watch on television is the same size as your kid's high school field...).

I once watched an interview of a celebrity who had an opportunity to sit in on the mandatory pre-race meeting for professional drivers in a well known auto race. The celebrity noted the tension in the room, with the kind of game faces, stern glares between rivals, and other competitive psych behaviors that you'd see between athletes and teams in more physical sports like basketball or football. It was a great insight from a seldom seen environment.

Optimal research combined with direct experience and the all important, transformative insight of location / place, provide what you need to build your story world and everything that inhabits it. These environments and 'real' people become the places and characters in your stories. For example, if you want to write stories that include the following, it would be hard to convey them accurately and, therefore, believably, if you'd never been in the environments themselves:

law office / court / jail

hunting / wilderness

businesses / companies / corporations / factories

classes of people — lower class, working class, white collar, blue collar

professional sports, school sports, recreational sports

backstage at a concert or show

driving a taxi

geological dig

racetracks (horse and auto)

on the ocean / in the ocean

a server in a fine restaurant / a server in a diner / a server in a truckstop

The key to incorporating research into a story is to take what you've lived or discovered and incorporate the experiences logically, seamlessly, accurately, and truthfully.

Here's a personal story about what being in a place or how something you've done can make a story come alive for you, and then for your reader:
Although I would not describe my life as having been full of adventure, my path has included some unique experiences, including being a paratrooper. When I teach The Way to Begin in a classroom, I take some time to describe my experiences because they are unique enough to serve as lessons in directly experiencing what you want to write about.

A paratrooper's experience begins before he or she 'is' a paratrooper; like any kind of specialty, paratroopers have to learn and train. In reality and as a fictional character, the young trainee going into jump school is a different person than he or she will be a year and a dozen or so jumps later. That experienced trooper goes through the following: getting into the harness of a parachute and attaching gear that can include full packs, sleeping bags, and a weapon; waddling in all that gear to sit and wait on the tarmac, then walking up the ramp of the plane, sitting among other young men and women as they fly to the jump zone; in the stick (a line of troopers when moving toward the door), standing and hooking the chute's static line (the nylon cord that when fully extended will pull the shoot out of its pack) to the cable strung above them along the length of the fuselage; shuffle-stepping to the door, the noise and rattling and wind, and seeing everyone turning and jumping out of the plane's door… It's all a bit overwhelming when you're new, something you get more used to with each jump. There's also noise at every facet — plane engines, the continuous clinking of metal connectors and nylon tie downs and netting along the inside of the austere planes; the smells of plane and jet fuel, engine exhaust; the unceasing drone of the props or jet engines, the smells of sweaty soldiers and what they might have eaten for breakfast or lunch, or the smell of those meals emanating from vomit bags of those unlucky enough to have made a poor meal choice prior to going on a bumpy flight, and on and on.

It is a unique environment and one that can't be accurately or emotionally conveyed by someone who hasn't directly experienced it. Yes, there are certainly experiences in which we cannot directly participate, but interviewing someone who has had the experience can get you insights that, when tied to the emotions and observations of your character, create riveting, revealing, suspenseful, dramatic scenes.

Review

- Ideas are incomplete and too unformed to be any kind of viable story;

- Competent writing and compositional skills are required to make the idea-to-story transition easier;

- Moving from idea to story begins with a catalyst, something(s) that begins to expand your idea into something of substance;

- Decisions about characters, places, and motivations are the catalysts;

- Decisions about story elements are what make a story possible, and that happens because the simplest definition of story is: **a description of actions, reactions, and consequences, all influenced by context**;

- Context is backstory and influences;

- What you are familiar with is a legitimate way to make decisions about your story, but not enough from which to *complete* a story; you must research, and the best research is to go, to be there, to do it; if you can't do it yourself, find people who have done it or actively do it, and ask them not just about the mechanics, ask them how the feel when they do it, what they see, hear, feel, and smell.

- The value of research is to take what you've discovered and incorporate it logically, seamlessly, accurately, and truthfully into the writing.

Decision Time
Going from idea to decisions

You have an idea of what kind of book or story you're ready to write, even if you aren't sure how to describe it. Let's break it down so we can start to really build your story. As we do this, know that these are not promises to yourself — you can change things, everything if you wish, but for now you're about to make some defining decisions that will get you to the point of putting words on paper or screen.

1 - Make a general decision about the kind — not the genre — of book or story you're ready to write. What do you like? Do you like humor, do you believe your story will be best presented as funny, like the works of Carl Hiaasen or Christopher Moore? Is it going to be romantic, or scary? Is it a true story, your family history, memoir, or something about a historic incident?

You may have either planned on what kind it's going to be, or have always wanted to write the same 'kind' of story that you like to read. Now is the time to commit. (BTW, if you're writing a children's, young-adult reader or teen story, everything about The Way to Begin still applies)

2 - NOW write this: "My story will be..." Use an adjective to finish this, a descriptor: funny, dramatic, scary, etc. Obviously this is not a long or complicated assignment. It's a commitment to a direction, and writing it should give you some confidence and a sense of control.

3 - Now be more industry specific by picking your book's genre. The publishing industry separates subjects into genres. Are you writing:

fiction

science fiction

historical fiction

modern romance

period or historical romance (period romance books with the swarthy, swashbuckling, muscular male and swooning female on the cover are often referred to as a bodice ripper), which tends to be more history-themed, a story that is one part romance, spy story, thriller, etc, and several parts period-based, i.e., the 1700s, 1800s, royalty, adventure, pirates, Indiana Jones, etc.

fantasy

crime

thriller

horror

biography

narrative nonfiction (any Jon Krakauer book, or Truman Capote's In Cold Blood, widely regarded as the first nonfiction crime book written as what's now called narrative nonfiction)

It's about to get more challenging — you will soon compose three to five sentences that describe your story, what I call the creative writing version of a ***log line***. We can relieve some of the pressure you may be feeling by reiterating that nothing you're doing is a promise (but it is a commitment!) — you can change your log line later, but you've got to write it before we're done.

The log line or the pitch describes a film story in one sentence. The movie industry focuses on finance and brevity, in that its movers and shakers live by 'time is money,' and much value — right or wrong — is placed upon the ability to relay the meat of a film through a short statement describing the film's **essence**. If you're lucky enough to get someone in the right position in Hollywood to listen to your movie idea, you've got to interest them — hook them — in no more than a few seconds and in as few words as possible.

The creative writing version of the log line approach can be an invaluable, foundational writing tool, especially for new writers, because it forces a writer to refine, define, and focus on the *core* of a story. Don't be fooled — the log line's handful of sentences can be extremely difficult to write, because simplicity takes great effort.

Here are three examples of a log line (you may be aware of these stories but haven't read or seen them; that's ok, because you can judge how accurate they are by reading them first and reading them after):

Rocky - An unranked club fighter gets the chance to fight the heavyweight champion.

Alice in Wonderland - A little girl follows a talking rabbit down a rabbit hole and discovers a wondrous and sometimes dangerous fantasy world.

Titanic (the movie) - a teenage aristocrat falls in love with a likable, lower class gifted artist who keeps her safe after the ship they're both on hits an iceberg and begins to sink.

Romeo and Juliet - Two teenagers fall in love despite their feuding families.

What matters in each of those log lines is *that's* the story's core. All the nuance and backstory and dreams and thoughts and settings and digressions and actions and everything else about those examples really don't matter at the log line stage.

The Way to Begin uses four to five steps to develop a creative writing log line. The results give you succinct information you can use to begin writing. It's not fair to call this process 'simple,' but it is much simpler than you might expect.

Review

- You've made a decision about what kind of story your writing (funny, sad, revealing, etc.)

- You've decided your story's publishing genre (science fiction, romance, historical, mystery, fantasy)

- Your about to decide several elements you will use to construct a three to five sentence log line to describe your story.

The beginning steps

Your decisions about how to complete these next four statements are the beginning steps toward your story's opening pages. Here they are as a group, after which I'll provide examples for each step:

This story is about… *a person/people (or other 'entity', to be explained in a bit)*, what, time, or place*

And he / she / they… *discovers, acts, receives, is confronted by*

And because of that… *something will happen*

Which means that / And that will… *force something, change something, create something, destroy something… and lead to CONSEQUENCES and a RESOLUTION(S)*

***NOTE:** for the first statement, a 'who' can be an animal, if that animal is integral to the story or, as has happened over the last few years, if the story is told by or from the animal's perspective. Two excellent examples are Garth Stein's novel *Racing in the Rain*, and the private investigator and his dog *Dog On It* series by Peter Abrahams. When presented well, the 'who' can also be a space alien, a ghost or spirit, or… (well, it's your decision)

Examples

Crime and thrillers

"This is about — Harry, a janitor

"And he — finds a body at the school where he works

"And because of that — his life is in danger

"Which will lead to — Harry having to prove his innocence and stay safe"

The book's log line:

Harry is a long time, well liked school janitor, but after he finds the principal's dead body one night in the school's basement, he becomes both suspect and the killer's next target.

General fiction

"This is about — Lori, a florist and widow

"And she — is about to file bankruptcy

"And because of that — everything about her life will change

"Which will lead to — Lori having to make decisions about her suddenly complicated future, about her eleven year-old daughter, her ninety-year-old mother, and about the man who wants to marry Lori."

The book's log line:

Opening a flower shop seemed like a good idea at first, but after Lori's husband died unexpectedly and the economy tanked, she was ready to file for bankruptcy, but then love showed up in the form of the nicest delivery guy she'd ever met and complicated her life even more.

The author's mantra for writing Lori's story is: "My decisions lead to Lori's challenges, lead to Lori's decisions, lead to consequences and resolutions."

Nonfiction, biography, and informative work

"This is about — Constantinople, which was the capital city of the Roman/Byzantine Empire

"And its — fall from greatness

"And because of that — it lost its position as the 'new' Rome

"Which led to — the end of the Middle Ages and the beginning of the Renaissance"

The book's log line:

Constantinople was the world's most robust city of its time, until the world changed faster than the city could adapt, and it figuratively crumbled as the Renaissance arose.

NOTE about biographies, memoirs, and how-to

While some biographies and memoirs are the record of an entire life, commercially published titles are also the result of an experienced writer who specializes in the bio/memoir genre, often in partnership with a deeply involved editor. No matter the author, though, there are often critical elements or aspects of the subject's life that control the narrative. One example is the spectrum of books about Steve Jobs, from business books about how to do business presentations like Jobs did, to Walter Issacson's expansive biography. Importantly, biographies and memoirs are not just a documentation of what someone accomplished under what circumstances, they must also reveal and explore — in the same way as fictional characters — the humanity, or lack of it, that shaped their subjects' lives. The more technical aspects of biographies include footnotes and sources, but as you study those genres, you can still start forming your idea about presenting your subject's story. In my opinion the three volumes about President Lyndon Johnson by Robert A. Caro demonstrate the work of a master biographer.

How-to books remain hugely popular, and for every individual thing that can have a how-to written about it, there can be dozens of titles. The separator is the style and the approach. The now widely distributed and deep trove of "…for Dummies" titles are successful because of the consistent style and tone of each book, and each book's clarity in explaining whatever the reader might be looking for. The distinguishing features of how-to books include: the intended audience (beginner, professional, quest for mastery; casual user vs. career oriented); looking for solutions reader, self help, to supporting and/or understanding; and the generally inquisitive reader to the researcher. If how-to is your intention, the creative log line development is a great clarifier to get you started. REMEMBER, writing how-to books require you to be organized AND to write for your reader (just like the intentions of all other books).

Your Creative Log Line
Knowing your story

Let's go over each statement you're going to create. Remember the progression: "**My decisions** lead to my characters' challenges, **causing them to make decisions,** leading to consequences and resolutions."

1 -- This story is about: a person / people / entity, what, time, or place

Except for the Constantinople example, **This is about...** is best completed by inserting a **person** (at least for now while you're still finding your way), and that's because *people*, our story's characters, are the reason we read. Emotionally evocative animals, wild or domesticated, also fit here: dogs, cats, horses, birds, etc. But I stress people at the "This is about..." stage because even when we choose to enhance or escape our own lives and circumstances through reading, we do it by connecting to a story's living 'something' and empathizing with their circumstances (human, alien, demon, ghost, animal, or…), whether those beings live on this planet, in this time, or another planet and another time.

Few fiction or narrative nonfiction stories succeed without a being or beings at the core.

We are the centers of our universes (yep, plural, and a subject for a different book) and experience our existence from the center out. We *are* that center. But that means our story's characters are bound by that same limitation. Every character is the center of his, her, or its own universe, and can only experience life from their own center. This is the essence of writing from a character's point of view.

So you must KNOW your character:

- where your character is from

- what your character wants

- why your character wants (**why** is what drives character thought and action)

- what makes your character happy, sad, angry, etc.

- what he / she thinks of the world, of men, women, children, 'things' in all their various morphs, i.e., how/what she thinks about attractive people, ugly people, skinny, heavy, black, white, loud, quiet, Asian food, reality TV, cars, school, the web...

And when you know that, then you know what your characters: wear, eat, live, read, watch, listen to; you'll know their habits, hobbies, you'll know it all.

As you create your characters, you'll begin to understand how locations, circumstances, and fate (again, you create it all) also become characters. I think of plots, timelines, backstories, fate, and pacing as roadmaps for your story's world; there are the maps you create, then maps are created by your plot, and maps your characters create — or think they create!

Here's another storytelling rule borrowed from filmmaking: nothing presented in your story is insignificant. People who make or study films understand that the briefest of shots, which may seem innocuous or innocent, almost always convey foreshadowing, a hint of something relevant that will be revealed later.

My personal example, my own "Ah-ha!" moment as I watched it unfold is from the 1982 film Poltergeist (and now you have an idea of just how old I am), and I'll try to describe this scene without giving away what it foreshadows so you can research it yourself if you wish.

Early in the story a family's pet canary dies, the children place it in a cigar box 'coffin' and after a family funeral bury it in the backyard. Later in the film, as the family has work done on the home a bulldozer tears out the home's built-in pool and there is a brief, several-seconds close up of the canary's cigar box coffin being dug up and tumbling out of the soil.

Quick and at first apparently insignificant, that scene foreshadows reason why ghostly things are happening to the family, even though the scene itself is never referred to by any of the story's characters.

The relation of that technique to creative writing is that while there are indeed sentences in which all you're apparently doing is writing, like this, "…she made a left turn and parked in front of the diner…" which seems only to describe a brief, innocuous moment in your created universe, the underlying significance is *why* she chose that particular route to get there, *why* she had to go there in the first place, etc.

The significance may only be known to you (backstory), that a better route may have been closed due to construction, or it may be she's always taken that particular route for the thirty-two years she's been meeting her friend there for lunch, or… it's where the stalker who would insert himself into the fabric of her life just happened to be standing on that day, that moment she pulled up and parked.

Nothing you present to your reader is insignificant, ever.

Take some time now to think about the layers of your story's characters and plot. Make some notes, doodle, and let your imagination, subconscious, or research all come together to birth your story:

- contemplate your character's(s') motivations
- contemplate the catalysts of and on your plot — character actions; natural phenomena; synchronicity; coincidence; omnipotence

As you do the exercise remember that if you know:

where your character is from

what your character wants

why your character wants that / those

...then you'll know what makes your character(s) happy, sad, angry, sloppy, organized, skeptical, lackadaisical... Those traits and emotions are directly connected to how your characters think of themselves, and how your characters perceive, correctly or incorrectly, how people regard them. You'll also begin to understand and see in your mind's eye 'what' your characters are. If you haven't decided some of those already, or if in creating them your vision of them is still fuzzy, look at them and observe that the character is: old, young, skinny, overweight, white, olive, black, loud, quiet... etc.

And the last part of the above paragraph is an opportunity to touch upon something related to developing character and how a character perceives himself vs. how that same character is perceived objectively.

What follows may at first be uncomfortable to read but is necessary so you as a writer know how to convey any truth in a story, and to help you realize that without truth you have nothing. These descriptors are innocuous and safe: old, young, skinny, overweight, etc. But, to create characters that live and breathe for readers, a character's own descriptions of people would require words that convey that character's subjective perspectives, using his or her own words and cultural references that could include the innocuous, safe terms, but more likely include words crude, base, or demeaning: fat, gay, fag, skinhead, punk, bitch, moron, stupid motherfucker, dickhead, whore, wetback, punk, asshole, saint, guru, etc.

The truth is often uncomfortable, whether writing it or reading it, but is always in everyone's best interests.

As you do this exercise — **This story is about...**(a who) — refer to everything above and ruminate on it all. You'll be surprised at how much you know as you write character descriptions and begin to plot your story: what they wear, eat, where they live, where they go, why they go there, how they get to places, what they read, what they watch, what they watch it on, how they speak, how they think, their habits, hobbies.

And now, with all of that presented to you in such a this-way-or-the-highway way, the opening pages you're going to create DO NOT HAVE TO BE ABOUT THAT PERSON. Just thought I'd get that somewhat confusing revelation out here now, so I can explain it in detail later. For now, concentrate on the 'who' of 'This story is about' and write for a while. Write more than you think you need. Your first 'This story is about' will be brief and succinct (eventually), but the more you know about that character the more succinct you'll be when you describe him, her, or it.

2 -- And he/she discovers, acts, receives, is confronted by...

We're deciding — at a very general level — a 'big' thing that will last for the entire story, even though you may not know right now just how that thing will play out, how it will affect the story, the characters, or the timelines.

And, like everything I'm presenting to you, that 'thing' can be anything, from an object to a situation to an emotion to an event: falling in love, an atomic explosion, exposure to typhoid, signing second mortgage documents, having a baby, kidnapping a baby, hearing a lie, hearing the truth, discovering a new planet, stealing a candy bar...

In our general fiction example, Lori's story, "And she — is about to file bankruptcy," is an event, a choice (perhaps voluntary, perhaps not), and a situation which has multiple, long lasting consequences and ramifications. A chart of how a bankruptcy affects someone's life would be massive, with layers of practical, psychological, emotional, current, and future consequences.

As you write your story, that discovery/act/confrontation/choice/etc., may become a distant memory by the time the story ends, may become almost a footnote, or may be the thing that brings the story to a conclusion, but its importance is huge, because the path that leads to your story's figurative or literal last two words — The End — begins with that discovery / act / confrontation / choice / etc.

3 -- And because of that, something will happen, which will create or destroy something (literally and/or figuratively), and lead to consequences and resolutions.

…Because *something* is always there, by choice, by logic, or by fate. And whenever something happens — a 'cause' — something else happens as a result — an 'effect.'

In the crime and thrillers example, Harry the janitor's discovery of a body leads to a 'something will happen' situation, in that his life is in danger (because the killer is watching him). In Lori's story, her 'something will happen' — her life will change — is a much broader something and ripe with possibilities which, for her story example, include the effects of the bankruptcy on every aspect of her life and the consequences of those effects (and how she chooses to deal, or not deal, with everything; a contemporary, sad example is if she turns to opioids, alcohol, or any other number of ways to relieve her emotional pain).

You are not yet committed to your final step of the creative equation — the consequences or conclusion — but you are very close to deciding the end of your story.

Knowing the end of your story is the biggest contributor to your story's beginning. Your story's conclusion is your story's beginning in the sense that everything that begins flows to its end. To get to the ending you must lay the foundation, the path, seed your plot with those incidents that take the reader to the end. Regardless of how you feel about life and death, spirituality, agnosticism, or religion, as a writer *you* are fate, and you best serve yourself when you know how your story ends. You create everything, every sign, character decision, accident, heads-or-tails result, every fall in or out of love, and so, as the creator of the universe you *know* how the story ends. You can play with the words, craft and create a plot full of misdirection or obstacles, or give a character multiple personality disorder at the mid-point of your story... but you have to know where you're going to get there.

Another assignment:

Write your 'idea' in as many paragraphs as you need, but try to keep it to one page. Read what you've written then strike through the words or sentences that are tendrils, that have too much information, that distract, are too wordy. Take what remains and write a new paragraph, add two or three words if you need to, or rewrite entire sentences. Now review and take out as many adjectives and adverbs as you can without weakening your almost-formed premise, and keep doing this until you have three to five COMPLETE sentences (because sentence fragments and bullet-speak are for weenies and poorly educated copywriters).

Use the answers to also discover what you don't know about the externals of your story, i.e., locations, industries, history(ies) / timelines.

Author-Worthy Prose
Elevate the quality of your writing

> The difference between adequate writing and author-worthy prose is work

Author-worthy prose means you write at a professional level. That's it. It's not a debate, not something to be nuanced in wide ranging philosophical discussions — "Well, what is professional, really?" (I direct you back to the earlier "I drive a truck" vs. "I am a truck driver" explanation.)

It means you are beyond capable, beyond the basics of punctuation and grammar, sentence structure, character development, dialog, plotting and pacing.

It means that when you write, your final draft is polished, conveys information, evokes feelings, and makes the reader *want* to continue to read what you've written.

And you never take your knowledge or skill for granted.

Writing author-worthy prose is hard work. It's not back-breaking hard, not steel worker or emergency responder hard, not physically exhausting hard... but it's hard work.

It becomes more challenging as the writer improves, because the writer is always elevating her own standards.

And writers love to get better.

For a new writer, all of that can be intimidating, enthralling, or both. But you can do it. I'm giving you some help, but you should understand and accept how much work it takes. Here's one of my favorite examples about professional-level performance. It's a sports story, although perhaps not quite what you expect. The takeaway is at the end and yes, it relates to creating author-worthy prose.

Steve Kerr is a nine-time NBA champion. He's had a stellar, multiple championships career, starting as a player with the Chicago Bulls, playing alongside

Michael Jordan and coached by another legend, Phil Jackson; won two more titles playing with the San Antonio Spurs; won multiple titles as the Golden State Warriors coach; and in 2024 he coached the U.S. Men's basketball team to a gold medal.

It barely needs stating that professional athletes have gifts, a life tapestry woven of inherent hand-eye coordination skills, natural athletic ability, instinct, and other foundational talents, along with smart decisions, luck, fate, and strong work ethics.

Strong work ethics.

During game six of the 1997 Bulls' championship series, with 28 seconds left in the game and score tied at 86, and the championship if the Bulls win, Kerr took an inbound pass from Jordan and hit a 17-foot jump shot. It put the Bulls in the lead 88-86 with five seconds left. Another great play from Bulls' Scotty Pippen sealed the victory in those last few seconds, but it was Kerr who won that game.

During a time out before Kerr's winning shot, coach Jackson and Michael Jordan had devised the play to draw the Utah defenders to Jordan, who would then pass to an open Kerr for the shot. After the game an interviewer talked to Kerr about the shot, the pressure of that got-to-make-this moment, and asked how Kerr did it.

I'm paraphrasing here, but Kerr's response was, "It was just like the thousands of jump shots I took growing up."

Thousands of shots. Almost certainly not an exaggeration considering by the time Kerr turned pro he'd been playing basketball since he could hold a basketball.

Thousands of shots. It is more likely now that it's tens of thousands.

Thousands of words.

The more you do something the better you can become at it. The more you do it, the easier it becomes to *continue* to do it. When you read a book, those words are the culmination of someone who has worked hard, everyday, sometimes every moment, to be able to write the book that interested an agent, an editor, then a publisher, and eventually resonated with you and thousands of other readers.

Hit that jump shot, take that curve at 180 m.p.h., create the iPhone, film the hit movie, hit the bullseye, win the Pulitzer... Or damnit, just please yourself.

The first key to writing author-worthy prose:

Write everyday

Everyday.

Study, go to classes, teach yourself, read, read, read, and write everyday.

I noted this earlier — writing one page with one-inch margins, double-space, 12 point, Times New Roman, results in approximately 350 or more words.

In a day, one page.

In a week that's a decent sized article.

A month, *just one month*, that's a short story.

Six months, you have a novella (long short story or short novel).

One year, you have over 120,000 words — a book-length manuscript.

Some writers set a daily goal of words written; your daily goal could be that 300-400 words mentioned above, or it could be one, two, three or more pages every day. Other writers commit to a daily period of time instead of a numbers-based goal, an hour, four hours, or more to write as many words as that time produces. Many writers give themselves an additional mandate, to commit to that one or several hours a day, and whether anything gets written during that time or not, the writer doesn't get out of her chair until that time is over.

Whatever else it takes to help you get to that everyday goal, do it. Only you have to know, and when you're teaching your own how-to-write class or giving that interview to Poets & Writers magazine, you can share that you always wore your favorite hat, shirt, smoked a pipe, or repeated a personal mantra.

Each day you write, you reinforce and use everything else you're doing to become a writer. Writing everyday is where all the books and articles you read, everything you learn, everything you teach yourself, become your words on paper.

Here's a suggested mantra: **Do it one day at a time, EVERYDAY at a time.**

Second key to writing author-worthy prose:

Don't settle for anything less than the best from yourself

Don't settle. If you want to become an author-worthy writer, don't settle for anything less than the best you can do.

It can be tiring to write, edit, rewrite, edit, rewrite. I know it, all good writers know it. We all do it because we know it's the only way to do it.

Well, it's the only way to do it if you want to write like a pro.

There is absolutely nothing wrong with writing to please only yourself, or writing your family history to share with family and close friends. It's a challenge for up-and-coming writers to get past the, "I think for what I want it's fine. It's not as if it's going to be a best seller or anything like that."

Yep, that's correct, whatever is written within those parameters will never be a best seller, but visions of best seller should never be the motivation or reason to write something.

The "it's fine" attitude is disappointing because it conveys that the writer knows the writing could be better, yet is satisfied with less than better… but still expects someone to read it. That sentence reads a bit more snooty than I intend, and I truly don't want it to sound disdainful because completing a first manuscript is a significant achievement.

But this is the 'how to write author-worthy prose' section, and surrendering to "I think it's fine" is not the way to a create something author-worthy.

Third key to writing author-worthy prose:

Work to be better

Write, get it on paper, edit to make what you've written better, and write the next draft better than the previous draft. Few among us are true prodigies, which is why most of us have to work hard to produce great work. 'Work to be better' is connected to 'write everyday,' because you want to be a better writer — writing everyday is necessary, working to be better is the goal.

Great stuff, you might be thinking, but **HOW DO I ACTUALLY BEGIN?**

Every artist in every medium has a singular, personal way to begin. The guidance here is derived from a study of my own work and those of authors who influence me. I tend to begin fiction, nonfiction, stories, or articles in the same way. It may not be what works for the rest of your writing career but it is effective and, objectively, the way many stories begin (as you'll see from examples later).

Essentially, it works.

To begin, focus on a moment, preferably a character's moment, whether that moment's character is a person, people, a place, a time, or an incident

A shovel hits the hard surface of something that shouldn't be there.

The gambler who has bet his and his wife's life savings on a horse as it finishes first… or last…

This sentence, "Trevor's shovel hit something hard in the dirt" may be an adequate sentence, and the lack of information is intriguing — is Trevor a gardener? Landscaper? Mafioso? — so I'll read some more, but give me more to begin with. When that shovel hits the hard surface of something that shouldn't be there, follow that opening moment with words and context that provide the feeling of that instant, not just the feel of the shovel smacking something, but more, the feel of the day or night, the setting, and Trevor's emotions, thoughts and actions:

"The shovel's blade hit something foreign, hard, a *tink* coming out from what should have been smooth, rich garden soil. Nothing too troubling with that, could be a piece of broken glass, could be a damn rock. But what troubled Trevor now as he wiped sweat from his eyes and struggled to get the shovel's blade under whatever it was, stabbing the soil, yanking the blade out, moving it, again, and again, was that the shovel seemed to be making the outline of a coffin."

Set-up the moment with which you'll open your story by thinking about the moment that came before it! Often the moments just before something special, remarkable, or dreadful, are great plotting and character-related opportunities. Think of the moments you experienced just before something unexpected happened in your life, or the moments leading up to something you expected to go one way but it didn't, or went exactly as you envisioned it would: as a kid running up grandma's front steps; the building anticipation of meeting the boss to ask, to demand a raise; or those thoughts just before you said, "I do."

You're not writing a diary. Compose sentences that convey emotional, intellectual, and *manipulative observation*, a phrase that means use words and phrasing to spin the reader in the direction you wish the reader to go — make the reader scared, sad, incredulous, awestruck, or mislead the reader (to mislead successfully, the writer has to rectify or reveal the misdirection later in the story, that moment when the reader either literally or figuratively slaps himself on the head, like what happens to most of us when we read Stephen King).

Anyone can describe a person shoveling dirt or doing something as simple as drinking water. But you're a creative writer, and your story succeeds or fails in large measure by how your words make the reader *feel* and *imagine*. Give me the context of the moment. A man drinking water conveys what he's doing, but if he 'gulps' the water, that conveys a little something more.

The through line (and plot)

We've covered how to refine and develop your idea into a definitive understanding of your story, how to create realistic characters to populate your story, and how to choose where to begin.

Now meet the through line, a concept of how to weave character thoughts, backstory, asides, and anecdotes into your writing; how to write in a way that makes characters as real as us.

We carry our life story with us in every moment. So do our story's characters. Our actions, reactions, thoughts, and emotions manifest from our experiences, linking our past moments to this moment. Does every moment we've ever experienced manifest in everything we do? No. Do we always have an experience that informs something we're going through? Nope.

We store situations, things we do, things done to us, what we see, hear, smell, dream, and they all inform us, usually when appropriate, occasionally when inappropriate (like something happening in church that evokes a memory or thought that makes you giggle uncontrollably). Sometimes we don't understand why we have a flash of something, a memory, a feeling, an immediate compunction to get out of or into a situation, and we only know why after, or never know why at all.

A woman who grew up in an abusive home and who sees or experiences abuse as an adult will react differently than someone who does not have that personal, direct connection to that trauma. If she's waiting for the commuter train and witnesses a man verbally or physically abusing a woman, the thoughts, memories, and actions — or lack of action — reveal volumes about her. In the reality of existence, we could never know her thoughts or how what she witnesses triggers connections to her past, unless she shared them with us.

As a writer, **you** reveal it all to us. And that's the key to how and where you weave things into your writing. You are the creator of all those moments, and you share, reveal, and present them as they happen to your character. You balance the logic of when a character's moment or connection to a recent incident occurs — as the woman sees another woman being abused — against the creative writer's or journalist's decisions about describing the moment or connection.

Here's the relevance of all that to the through line concept. Recall the first statement of your creative log line: This story is about…

Your through line is the complete statement: This story is about Jacky (the woman waiting for the commuter train).

In electronics, devices that measure the frequency of a tone (a sound) display a sine wave, a line that repetitively rises and descends relative to a flat baseline, like this:

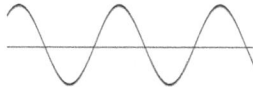

The baseline line is your through line; the wavy line represents digressions, takeoff points for a moment of memory, a snippet about Uncle Tommy at a party, a child's baptism. Sometimes the sine wave has large peaks and valleys, sometimes it's barely a sine wave at all, but no matter where it goes it always returns to the through line.

Because this story is about Jacky, she is your through line, the one element of your story that you always return to. She is a straight line that runs from your first page to your last, even when you're not writing about her. No matter how far you roam, no matter whether you digress into Jacky's grammar school years, her first job, her first husband, her mom's funeral, her dad's mistress, her friend's lover, her observation of what's happening on the train platform, wherever and however long you go, you eventually must return to Jacky 'now.'

This is a bit of a simplification, because we all know stories are about multiple characters, some lasting the story's length, others making only brief appearances. Those characters' lives have their own through lines and digressions, but without a very good reason, a story's through line should focus on one, or no more than a few, characters.

Like Jacky's through line, when you move from a different character's present moment into a reaction, day dream, remembrance, or other meandering, you eventually have to come back to them.

Note: whether your story is about one or one-hundred characters, there is rarely more than one through line (if it's a story about a team or an Army platoon, that group is the through line). Multiple waves = multiple characters, and the highs, lows, and lengths of the waves would vary for different digressions. Keep in mind this is a visual concept rather than something you should 'do.'

An important note about writing your character's moments within moments: don't mix characters' points of view at the same time. Using Jacky and the incident on the platform, for example, this —

"The man grabbed the woman's arm and yanked her to him. Jacky flinched, as if he had grabbed her too. The uncontrollable reflex made her feel vulnerable, then angry."

— should not be followed with the internal voice or perspective of a different character: "Harry, the hardhat worker standing near the couple, thought the man was a little rough."

Jacky can observe the hardhat worker, which means that you write *her* observation of him, but switching points of view is confusing and reveals a newbie mistake. If the entire scene is written from an omnipotent point of view, however (and I don't recommend you do that at this stage of your writing education), there is more leeway in popping into and out of different characters' heads.

Rather than write an omnipotent point of view, consider opening with descriptions, backstory and context which directly relate and lead to a character's introduction another page or two later. A favorite author of mine, Richard Russo, is a master of positioning a place as a character, weaving the location's macro and micro history into the lives of the people who live there (because, as you now know from earlier sections, *where we are* and *where we come from* are large parts of *who we are*). I strongly recommend all his books to writers and readers, and nothing serves as a better example of place as character than the opening of his book *Everybody's Fool*. We read several long, descriptive paragraphs of the town's history and local cemetery before we even meet one of the book's main characters. Here's the opening paragraph:

Hilldale Cemetery in North Bath was cleaved right down the middle, its Hill and Dale sections divided by a two-lane macadam road, originally a colonial cart path. Death was not a thing unknown to the town's first hearty residents, but they seemed to have badly misjudged how much of it there'd be, how much ground would be needed to accommodate those lost to harsh winters, violent encounters with savages and all manner of illness. Or was it life, their own fecundity, they'd miscalculated? Ironically, it amounted to the same thing. The plot of land set aside on the outskirts of town became crowded, then overcrowded, then chock-full, until finally the dead broke containment, spilling across the now-paved road onto the barren flats and reaching as far as the new highway spur that led to the interstate. Where they'd head next was anybody's guess...

Here are two more openings, the first from *Get Shorty*, Elmore Leonard's classic, humorous crime novel, followed by my own narrative nonfiction work, *Move To Fire*, the true story about a boy paralyzed in an accidental shooting by a defective gun.

Study each sentence and note what's in it literally and figuratively — emotions, descriptions, *manipulative observations*, the choice of words, the construction of the sentences, the active verbs. Also note that the main through lines of each book's main characters — Chili and Brandon — are there from the beginning. They each begin with a specific moment and weave information and digression into the through line.

Get Shorty:

When Chili first came to Miami Beach twelve years ago they were having one of their off-and-on cold winters: thirty-four degrees the day he met Tommy Carlo for lunch at Vesuvio's on South Collins and had his leather jacket ripped off. One his wife had given him for Christmas a year ago, before they moved down here. Chili and Tommy were both from Bay Ridge, Brooklyn, old buddies now in business together. Tommy Carlo was connected to a Brooklyn crew through his uncle, a guy named Momo, Tommy keeping his books and picking up betting slips till Momo sent him to Miami, with a hundred-thousand to put on the street as loan money. Chili was connected through some people on his mother's side, the Manzara brothers. He worked usually Manzara Moving & Storage in Bensonhurst, finding high-volume customers for items such as cigarettes, TVs, VCRs, stepladders, dresses, frozen orange juice... But he could never be a made guy you see, hear what you hear, feel what you feel, even imagine what you imagine.

- **Be direct and specific when you describe.** This description, "The book was old," is passive and weak, because your "old" book and my "old" book are very different old books. If that old book matters to you as the creator of the universe in which it resides (and it should matter) then pull me into that universe by presenting that book with all it represents, physically, emotionally, and intellectually.

Tips on opening sentences

Try not to begin like this: "She was tired…"

She was tired might be adequate based on how you finish the sentence, but the word 'was' is an indicator of passive writing, the way most people write in a diary, note, or memo. 'Was' is often part of a description conveying information, but offers little energy when used to describe an action or convey the current state of someone or something. Active writing *propels* a story, because the reader is in the story's moments, the characters' moments. Was does have its uses. Re-read the Trevor and the shovel example, or the first sentence of Get Shorty's second paragraph.

These two simple sentences are classic examples of passive vs. active writing:

Passive: The postal worker was attacked by the dog. (think of this as a re-telling, something in the past)

Active: The dog attacked the postal worker. (think of this as a 'now')

Now the passive 'was' is joined by 'of':

Passive: He was mesmerized by the colors of the sunset. (an arm's length description)

Active: The sunset's colors mesmerized him. (those colors are mesmerizing him now)

Work to find and, when appropriate (because, yes, sometimes the words 'was' and 'of' are the best choice for a sentence), rewrite 'was' and 'of' sentence construction.

One way to eliminate the 'was' passive sentence:

For 'was,' as in *The postal worker was attacked by the dog*.

First, delete 'was' and rearrange the phrase after it— "*attacked by the dog*" — so that the article and noun, "the dog," now lead to the verb for what the dog *did*, "attacked:" *The dog attacked…*

Now take what was originally the beginning of the sentence, "the postal worker," the target of the dog's attack, and place it at the end of the sentence: *The dog attacked the postal worker.*

When 'was' and 'of' are used in the same sentence:

First, understand that 'of the' constructions — colors *of the* sunset, the wives *of the* shah, the armies *of the* king — are easily flipped with a possessive apostrophe. A brief but important explanation of the possessive apostrophe vs. plural s (no apostrophe) follows.

Using 'of the' denotes possession, something that *belongs* to a noun. Which colors? The *colors that belong to the rainbow*. Which armies? The *armies that belong to the king*.

Creating more active-possessive prose removes the invisible middle man, as if someone stands between the author and reader, relaying the story information to readers. The 'of' and 'was' in passive writing separates what's possessed from its possessor. Changing passive 'of' simply requires a flip and a possessive apostrophe on the noun: the *sunset's colors*; the *shah's wives*; the *king's armies*.

BUT NOTE! The change from passive 'of' (the armies of the king) to active possession (the king's armies) only works with the possessive apostrophe, and knowing when and how to use that apostrophe correctly bedevils otherwise educated writers to this day. An apostrophe-s at the end of an object denotes possession of what follows that object: the president's message; *Frank's jacket; Betty's convertible; the building's exits*

A plural s — no apostrophe — is used for multiples of something: *all the past presidents attended; the sunsets have been gorgeous this week.*

A helpful reminder for how and when to use a possessive apostrophe is to think of its shape as a small hook that takes possession of what follows it. You may, however, have spotted something in the prior sentence that seems the opposite of what I just described. The exception to the possessive apostrophe is the word 'its.' When pointing out something — *its eyes; its claws, its power* — there is no apostrophe, due to the contraction of 'it is' which is *it's: it's cold, it's hot, it's confusing*.

And when confronted with a plural possessive, different style guides pick one of two ways to do a possessive plural: an apostrophe after the plural s — *the students' classrooms*; and plural s followed with an apostrophe s (rarely favored but technically correct): *all the stores's computers went down.*

And let's close this too brief wordsmith section with…

Strive to simplify and use better verbs instead of adverbs: "He sighed," rather than "He sighed heavily." Choosing the best verb is often better than adding an adverb. You could write "He drank the water greedily until the bottle was empty," but it's better to choose active verbs, words that evoke images: "He gulped the water, emptying the bottle."

Allow me these repetitions:

To begin, focus on a moment, a character's moment, whether that character is a person, or people, a place, a time; don't write in a diary. (This is what separates many developing writers from accomplished writers.)

Compose sentences that convey emotional, intellectual, and manipulative observation:

- **Strive to describe.**
- **Avoid passive descriptions.**
- **Creative writing is active. You don't just tell us a story, you include us;** your words trigger and stir up readers' emotions.
- **We want to see what you see, hear what you hear, feel what you feel, even imagine what you imagine.**

- **Choose the 'best' words to be active and descriptive, to paint the image for the reader**. These words, for example — flowed, flooded, crashed, dribbled, dripped, splashed, roared, erupted, gushed, sprayed, covered, pooled — all refer to or describe a state of water

Be specific

Even if you've never heard singer Carrie Underwood's hit song, *Before He Cheats*, this line is a great example of choosing just the right words: "I took a Louisville slugger to both headlights."

Arguably, baseball bat would have been harder to rhyme, and there are people who don't know that a Louisville Slugger is the most well known brand of baseball bat in the country. But… it's specific and works to convey an energy that 'baseball bat' just doesn't create.

The song's lyrics have other specifics: "Right now he's probably dabbing on three dollars worth of that bathroom Polo." Bathroom Polo refers to one of a collection of trial-sized colognes for sale from dispensing machines in the restrooms of some bars. Choosing to use the phrase 'bathroom Polo' works to convey something simultaneously relatable and tawdry. There are other stellar word and phrase choices in the song, including frisky…fruity little drink…carved…slashed…

Songwriters and musicians are great storytellers.

Choose the 'best' words, the words that convey more than meaning. These words all refer to water but evoke very different images or feelings: flowed, flooded, crashed, dribbled, dripped, splashed, roared, erupted, gushed, covered, pooled.

About plot

A plot is your story's roadmap that you create with stops, diversions, and sights to see along the way to your destination. If you have not had classes on plot development or haven't done any study of it yet, it doesn't negate anything in The Way To Begin, but you can't write your story if you don't know what plot is, how to develop it, and why it matters. If we were to enlarge and study the through line, we'd see that it's not a solid line but a series of sections, all different sizes, strung together. Your characters meet, think, make love, visit family, steal, die, time travel, flunk, sleep, wake up, all those different vignettes (one or more of every moment's three acts, coming/being/going) that create your story.

As I've stated previously, some writers start with a blank page and nary more than an opening sentence and away they go... but that's not the norm. You can try it, and if you feel compelled to just start writing, and using the methods you've learned here, gosh, have at it, but you'll almost certainly need to plot your story at some point. Study, read, take note of how your favorite books move you along, and take the time to learn about developing your plot.

Outlining is a well used tool of long form writing. Not necessarily the kind you might have had to create in school, not overly detailed, but essentially a set of directions for where the story goes and how it gets there. You can do it before or while you're writing a draft, before is better. For The Way to Begin method, I recommend making at least a few notes about where your story might go, getting your log line together, creating the opening pages, and then taking some time to plan your chapters and the story's path. Aside from helping you see where you're going, the outline also works as an encouragement -- looking at it gives you a sense that you at least know where you're going today, and makes it easier for you to write everyday.

You're a storyteller. Tell the story. Use all your tools, choose those verbs and active words, edit and rewrite, rewrite, rewrite, do all of the things that have come before and after this section, but remember to be a storyteller. Whether your style is terse, lean, flowery, or colloquial, 'tell' the story.

Especially in your early drafts, let your characters ramble on. Take your time escorting the reader down Main street. Let those nerves surge at the height of the rookie's first race, first chase, first end of the shift. From nature's colors to chemical reactions, let the story develop, let it wash over your readers.

Break your readers' hearts, reveal your character's deepest thoughts, spin your readers around to pull back the curtain and show the trick, or don't and just spring it on them.

Do yourself the favor of re-reading a favorite or influential book with your new-ish, discerning author's perspective, and study the word choices, sentences, and paragraphs that stir something within you. If you own the book, make notes on the pages.

Summary and final practicalities

Read, and study (Dreyer's English, The Elements of Style)

Your story is a chain of moments, a tapestry, or a line of dominos; use the analogy that works for you! **Create a chain of moments and judiciously present relevant information about those moments and/or the transitions from moment to moment.**

Life is a three act drama.

Know your characters.

To begin, focus on a character's moment (which can be a person, place, incident, or thing).

Use active, evocative verbs.

Compose sentences, paragraphs, and pages that convey emotional, manipulative observation.

Don't stop writing, and it's good to set a daily goal even if the goal is a little squishy, i.e., a period of time vs. a number of pages.

Complete your first draft, accept that it's a first draft and that you will be rewriting it (that means the first draft will be overwritten and in need of editing / rewriting — that's what first drafts are, and great writing comes after rewriting)

You'll learn to be objective about your own work. With study and dedication, you'll eventually be able to evaluate and competently edit your own sentences. And if you're lucky, someday you'll work with an editor who will then rip it all apart to make it even better.

Don't style; you don't have style; style will find you. Style develops as you master your craft. Both take time, mastery takes daily work, and from that daily work your style will emerge. Just work and your style will take care of itself.

Be realistic about what you're doing, why you're doing it, and your expectations.

Carry a notepad and a pen. You can use a phone or other digital device, but you'll find it easier when you have that idea or you've just seen or observed something, to be old school and jot it all down. Whether a few words or several sentences, get in the habit, because even the smartest of us can't always remember that one thing we really, really wanted to remember because we… um, because… Oh, just carry the pen and paper already.

Be quiet. Talking is not writing. Writers groups, organizations, and clubs are important because writing can be lonely, and only other writers can understand what you're trying to do. But, like the seduction of research, talking about writing is much easier than actually writing, so if you feel the need for being a part of a writers group, that's great, but keep in mind that writing requires, well, writing! And also be judicious about choosing who to share your work with and when. Don't show your early drafts to anyone, and don't share drafts with people who can't really help, which limits that to someone who is a more experienced writer than you (I'd still be cautious about that), or an editor.

Tomorrow is not your moment

It promises a new start, a restart, an "I'm going to conquer the world" opportunity, when everything will change as you embark upon your new journey to your breakthrough book…

Bullshit.

My apologies for being crass and a little harsh. Tomorrow certainly will come, and it does indeed present a new day and, now that you've read The Way to Begin, tomorrow does indeed present an opportunity to write in a way and with a verve that may carry you forward to your first complete manuscript. But I'm asking, close to pleading, *that you not wait*, because tomorrow also offers another day to read instead of write, play instead of write, work instead of write.

Write as soon as you finish reading the last words in this book. Start something. Rewrite your creative log line; make it solid, confident; memorize it; begin listing your characters' traits, the backstory and context.

Write your opening sentence, and the next sentence, and the next.

The hardest thing to do is start. Hell, that's why you bought or borrowed this book, so you could start, begin, perform an action that will validate what you KNOW, that you have a story worthy of a reader's time, whether one reader or one-thousand. The beginning is so important because performing an action, whether cleaning out the garage, doing three pushups, signing up for a writing class, or writing that first line of your story is the first step to feeling in control.

It is the moment you will long remember, the moment you will use to motivate yourself and write the next day, and the next, and for the rest of your life.

Tomorrow is *not* your moment. **Now** is your moment. Tomorrow could be filled with distractions or be as empty as a desert sky, while today is known. Today is now. You don't have to write a dozen pages, you only have to write 'something,' because if you at least write something, your tomorrow is much more likely to include more writing.

My wish for you is that you read these last few pages, take a few minutes to breathe, refresh, have coffee, tea, water, whatever, perhaps re-read parts of this book, re-read your favorite book or books but with a now more discerning eye, read with your now informed, new perspective on how to begin. Note the language, the weave of context and back story around the through line. Read the opening paragraphs of books you love, then write that first page of your own future book.

Don't judge yourself, don't second guess, don't stop after the fifth sentence to go back and rewrite the second sentence, just write and let it pour out until you get to the bottom of the page.

Do the next page if you can, do as many as you want.

But do that first page, because it may become the most important page you'll ever write in your writing life.

Write now.

It takes what it takes... and takes as long as it takes. That reads a little superficial, slightly vacuous, or as an unknown cowboy once said, "All hat and no cattle."

New writers get very anxious as they near completion of the first manuscript. It's so, so close. And it feels great, as it should, because it is a significant personal accomplishment, which can really only be appreciated by another writer.

But you know it's not done. It's a first draft, it needs the same effort in editing as it did in writing. And it will need, certainly, at least another and probably another edit. Multiple drafts are required, whether you're Alice Hoffman or you, before your manuscript sees the light of day as a book.

Don't think of it as a discouragement; instead, think of editing as another great accomplishment, because it means you have an actual complete manuscript to edit!

It takes as long as it takes. I've written 2,500-word articles in a week; I wrote my first book, The Way to Communicate, in a matter of months; but it took me three years of research interspersed with seven years of writing to complete *Move To Fire*. I had no idea it would take that long, but I couldn't have finished it any sooner.

It takes what it takes, so concentrate on the writing and not the calendar. Really.

Go write and make yourself (and me) proud.

#####

Michael W. Harkins

Michael W. Harkins is an author, screenwriter, artist, and occasional media consultant. His 2016 book, *Move to Fire - A family's tragedy, a lone attorney, and a teenager's victory over a corrupt gunmaker*, was the culmination of a ten-year project documenting the true story of a boy accidentally shot and paralyzed by a defective gun, and the attorney who won a $25,000,000 product liability judgment for the boy a decade later. The book received acclaim in 2016 as one of only nine independently published nonfiction titles to receive a starred review from Publishers Weekly. The book has been optioned and is in development as a feature film.

In 2023, *If Steve Then Steph*, an exclusive profile of Steve Jobs personal producer of 30 years, spent several weeks as an Amazon New No. 1 Top Seller.

In his 40-year creative career his work has appeared in Real Simple magazine, Thrice Fiction magazine, business publications, and his commentary has aired on NPR's All Things Considered. His music industry projects include concert and video production for dozens of performing and recording artists including Journey, Bruce Springsteen, the Police, Eric Clapton, Michael Jackson, and Prince.

He is a former adult literacy tutor, wildlife organization volunteer, and veteran of the Army's elite 82nd Airborne Division.

www.ingramcontent.com/pod-product-compliance
Lightning Source LLC
Chambersburg PA
CBHW020341010526
44119CB00048B/562